INDIANLAND

Copyright © 2017 Lesley Belleau

ARP BOOKS (Arbeiter Ring Publishing)
205-70 Arthur Street
Winnipeg, Manitoba
Treaty 1 Territory and Historic Métis Nation Homeland
Canada R3B 1G7
arpbooks.org

Book design and layout by LOKI.
Printed and bound in Canada by Friesens on paper made from
100% recycled post-consumer waste.

Interior cover image from: *This Is Indian Land* credited to Fungus Guy.

Original image: commons.wikimedia.org/wiki/File:This_Is_Indian_land_1.JPG

 Canada Council   Conseil des arts    MANITOBA ARTS COUNCIL
for the Arts   du Canada   CONSEIL DES ARTS DU MANITOBA

Canadä   Manitoba

ARP BOOKS acknowledges the generous support of the Manitoba Arts
Council and the Canada Council for the Arts for our publishing program.
We acknowledge the financial support of the Government of Canada
through the Canada Book Fund and the Province of Manitoba through the
Book Publishing Tax Credit and the Book Publisher Marketing Assistance
Program of Manitoba Culture, Heritage, and Tourism.

LIBRARY AND ARCHIVES CANADA CATALOGUING IN PUBLICATION

Belleau, Lesley, 1976 –, author
        Indianland / Lesley Belleau.

Poems.
Issued in print and electronic formats.
ISBN 978-1-894037-92-1 (softcover) — ISBN 978-1-927886-02-1 (ebook)

        I. Title.

PS8553.E45698I53 2017   C811'.6   C2017-905420-1
                                            C2017-905421-X

INDIANLAND

Lesley Belleau

A small heart born and brought home in my mother's
arms to the log house my daddy and his brothers built
on the land that I know is home. giiwewidoon.
They carried me home.

And when I left, you found me and carried me home.
g'zaagin: my heart is open to yours. Your breaths,
my babies, our life.

The beginnings and the ends of things and everything
in between. I am grateful.

CONTENTS

This is Indian Land

a bridge in the middle of
garden river reserve
summoning history
the same as an old brown finger would
to a child

we walk across it
trying to beat the train

old birds fly by
slowing

a trail left by raccoons
disappear somewhere under my
tattooed toes
not so brown but for the dirt
between them

when I was a child I would watch the bridge
and wonder what people thought of us here
in G.R.
in the middle of nowhere
with the loudest bridge in the world
a screaming bridge
wailing from one end to the other
THIS IS INDIAN LAND

but now I know why our bridge needs to
howl

why the birds slow over the bridge
why the eagles protect the small black statue
why the paint never fades or dulls or
disappears

because we are not in the middle of nowhere
after all

this is the war zone picket sign
the biggest picket sign
our bridge is
the middle of the war
every reserve is the middle of it
every brown face is howling
and those who are tired
I don't want to fight because nobody listens
it gets too hard and too long and too quiet
and nobody hears us anyway
and I am getting old and my body is dying

and so the bridge
speaks for us

here in wartime
when warriors are dying
and birthing
and working

when dinner needs to be made

the warrior words scream out
the howl of Indian Land
each lost voice
dead baby
stolen child
each woman lost to the streets
every man
who doesn't see the
thunder of our histories

THIS IS INDIAN LAND

Cornhusk Dolls

and we gathered.
baskets swelled into sunrise, and we gathered.
yarrow coloured our fingers, inhaled our sweat onto its spine.
a damp heat had started. Our men were still sleeping.
and we gathered
dawn pressing us closer to home. Your woman breath next to mine.
sister fingers scraped new root, drank hawthorn with our flesh
delivered summer buds and stems to the bitten bark. Baskets
swelled into sunrise, edged over the foothills, where our men
slept like the dead beside our babies wrapped in tanned deerskins
beside their cornhusk dolls that wore hanging pelts over their
        fading bodies.

sunrise, and we gathered.
yarrow greened our nails, seeped into our flesh
our footpads broke the earth into trial.
branches brushed over our cheeks, hands led us back.
our men waited for us.
raised their hands, hot with the sweat of bone, to pull the flap for us.
to pull us between fur and thigh, our baskets emptied by the
        doorflaps.
fur and thigh to break the dawn.
we gathered.
their breathbuds soft as sumac, their hands damp heat
our bodies lit between brown flesh and cedar boughs.

us women picked.
foxglove.
scarlet sage.
waterlilies.
juniper.
goldenrod.
trillium.
white gaura.
until we greened our nails.
smudged their fleshes on our palm-skins.
rubbed milkweed round and round and round our hands

necks, arms,
thick as the side-swell of moon
until we were whitened
gauzed over beside the lush hue of noon.

our babies were squashed against us
flattening our breasts under our bearclaw necklaces
scraping blood. ochre red.
washing our hands, we see a new boat on our shore
wide prints leading outward toward the slant of our hills.
we picked, waiting for the break of grass, to crouch and wait
pointed bone-ready for battle.
bone behind wrist, we picked.
and waited.
picked and waited
our babies chewing roots on our shoulders, until they slept.

we discovered them eating on smushed lakegrass
their necks as white as dead cattail tips
lips tipped red with chokecherry blood—
hushhushhushhushhushhushhushhushhushhush—
and pulled our babies closer, their cheeks as warm as the long, flat
rocks of agawa,
lined in red, ochred red.
we discovered them.
dead cattail tips.
red with chokecherry blood.
red, ochred red.
hush. Hush.
crouched and waited.
bone point hovered behind wrist
the wail of chejauk in our minds
the taste of an old song lined our throats.

and the grass split
tip division
vision shone
their faces edged in cedar fringes.
new people
pale hair hanging
skins reddened by the sun.
sagegrass.

Contact.
grass, sweetgrass stompled under
salmon stilled under northbound streams
new-sprung bluejays stitched to their branches
made quiet here by their arrival.
contact.
new trails stomped open
the buds of our healing bursting over shoreline muds
stems scattered into crooked patterns.
long black hair braiding fern
our breaths parting the open space of their footpaths
cheek against the earth
a caribou scent from somewhere near
feeding a mushroom edge in the mouths of our babies to silence them.

and quiescent grass grew scorched inside the cusp of summer
as they fell over hill into sunset.
bone points scraping earth
we stood and gathered our baskets as slow as ritual.

us women picked flowers waiting for our men to find them
our babies squashed closely
long, flat cheeks warmed against us.
red clay brushed against the rockwall
canoes edged along the
ledges of Superior.
palms wet with red earth
the sound of history smudging into porous sandstone.

waabigwan, waabigwan.
force your last beauty on us now before they steal our faces.
line our memories with your breaths
our spinewalls with your continuum.

waabigwan, waabigwan.
you are more than soft piles beside our birchbark platforms
and death posts.
force your last beauty on us
weave yourselves into our children's eyeskin.
sew our strength to our sinew
behind the rope of our spines, the memories of our elders.

the new people spoke with their hands together.
wild rice in their beards
calendula water steaming their cheeks.
gathered in a straight line.
we walked closer
the edge of our men's eyes watchful
the corners of the doorflaps
waiting for us.
the fire had burned low, yellowed itself.
they watched us.
the lines of our necks
curve of bearclaw drawing blood
the separation of flesh and sinew
the waft of burdock from our tongues.

we let the cattail mats fall behind us
crawled between fur and earth
released the deerskin from our flesh
where our men found us waiting to press them
between ground and skypoint and
mid-chant and hipbone
under teeth where we run claw to flesh to find marrow
soaking up their histories with our stomach flesh
the squish of skins between moons
the colour of their sweat dulled fire
a memory of creation.

we slept,
dreamed of scattering rock and ashes
and the thick trail of a turtle entering stream.

a grandmother birthed a brown baby that night
legs teepeeing outward
under a great white pine
and new-sprung birds awakened
and on stirred under the northern waters
and new sweetgrass edged into purity
and round and round her fingers wove the air
wet with sweat and old ash.

One over the other, through
round, loop and pull, tighten, tighten.
One over the other, through
round, loop and pull, tighten, tighten.
One over the other, through
round, loop and pull, tighten, tighten.

fingerpads slivered grey
basketing the tongue of the August wind into tight coils
coloured red thirst inside of a coyote song
or the sudden stir of a wet baby
falling against the earth.

and they watched us.
The lines of our necks
curve of bearclaw drawing blood
the separation of flesh and sinew
the waft of burdock from our tongues.
And they watched us as we gathered.
foxglove.
scarlet sage.
waterlilies.
juniper.
goldenrod.
white gaura.
watched.
as we gathered.

baskets scented our flesh, greened our fingers.
watched us.
their hands together
necks as white as dead cattail tips.
hands.
white-edged.

hands.
shhhh.
hands.

shhhh. shhhh.
squashed. squashed. squashed.
squaw shhh squaw shhh squaw hush
squaw hush squaw hush   squaw hush squaw hush   squaw hush
squashed. squashed. squashed.
shhhh. shhhh.
hands.
hands together
necks as white as dead cattail tips.
hands.
squashing.
red ochre
bearclaw tip drawing blood.
hush.
hush.

us women carved bone together
sharpened jagged ridges with a slice of rock.
sharp as the purity of daybreak
we carved around the children.

made boned flowers with the remnants
hid them in the tuck of our baskets
skewered long bone into points
jagged ridges smoothed quiet
waxed the husk with our sweat
with the oil from a newly dead hide
polished our carve of bone
remnants following the pull of breeze
until we could see our faces in the shine of our weaponry.
until we could see our faces in the shine of our bone.
blank.
until we moved closer
leaned in
afraid to breathe out to break the time of reflection
and mask our faces with the thrust of our breath.
blank.
until we leaned closer.
eyes sharpened into points
smooth faces edged into jagged ridges
carved into bristled bonemasks
buried silent by the shape of their countries.
our children chewed on rock-charred flowers
unable to see their mother's faces
lost above them.

agogwaazo, agogwaazo.
they sewed us together
blank as cornhusk dolls.

November: zoogipon

In darkness came the first snow. *Zoogipon.* November, the
lights of the city are off and I stand on my deck his words as
memory fading. *I will walk through fire with you.* I remember
loving him when I heard those words because in times of
great fire and turmoil, I always stood alone. I remember
wondering if I should believe these words. I thought of his
hands writing them to me. His long fingers, the scars on his
fingers, the pads thick with stories. I believed it because of
those strong hands. He was the kind to push the flametips
apart, sacrifice his body to walk beside me, and hold my hand
through the darkest times. But we knew no dark times then.
We were so new like the snow.   21

November, the burn of air in the lungs, the insistence of
winter. I prayed that night on my deck, too much wine,
cigarettes, loneliness. I prayed for God to bring him to me.
And he came. But humanity and reality hung on his chest like
a fresh kill. And I wanted to skin it with him. I did. But I
didn't expect the guts, the bloodshed, the waste and gore
falling at my feet.

Watching him, an ever-changing and steady orb. No home,
you fell at my feet and then left me just as quickly. Maybe you
belonged to some other place. Maybe I couldn't find you here.
In your leaving, I release you. In your changing, I return to
my own home, wrapped tight, breathing, still breathing.
Little faces like constellations. My belly throbbing your name.

How do I recede? No defence, no indignation and I am
offended as a woman who craves protection. The naming of
women rolling off you like slick sleeting numbness. The things
you won't accept in me you accept in others. The hypocrisy in

your living, I am driven so far from you, I cannot remember
your face. You, so demanding in my purity, my woman-bearing,
my heat.

This dark place you lay in, your penchant, that pull toward
you, the gravity of it, my own demons you eat for nourishing.

What you feed expands. Your hand is the feeder, your own
hand, the enemy's long blanket. Those scars that I loved
worked against my love. One soft bite and you receded as
easily as silt.

Yes, the laughing, the concessions, the pull and give of the
tide, the panting of the womb.
The thinking space has never been so wide.

These dark, hidden corners are our bread, our meat. We can
starve our bodies and fill it instead with thoughts. All these
thoughts.

We are little crumbs scattered on memory's ego, nibbling
ourselves to bleeding.

November and I find your shadow here, already broken by the
winter's light, too covered to find you again.

nikanendi.

Love(lessly)

Without the words wasted words all those words and
nights I poured myself into you. Thirty seven and I
handed the pulp of my heart, sacrificed it on your
pulpit, watched it expand to exploding until drowning,
and I was five years old again, begging my father to
love me, to let me sit on his lap, to turn those brown
eyes on me and see me, just see this little heart,
waiting.

G'zaagin. My heart is open to you.

Born like a sliced sturgeon, with a heart bleeding
opened and pulling all the splintered love-edges into
me. The slicing, my body, all those throbbing eggs
exposed under the drum of hands maneuvering the
body, the meat of me, your hunger.

When you came and sacrificed me, broke me with
those steady hands, I saw your white hands pulling
me out of the water and into your wide and laughing
mouth like I was still underwater. I hear the sounds
of your voice now from my memory of swimming
the caves and from the swimming of your daughter's
shape in my belly but you are full, my love stuck to
the walls of my belly like petroglyphs and still I
persist somehow, gills pulsing under the thick air.
I am still here when you are not.

Niigoshkaa: it is broken.

Lost, and the Snow

This snow.
Your mouth against mine
the snow falling
your tongue a soft witness of my heartbeat
your sucking it out of my tongue, those hands
on the back of my neck, my face
I am breathless and I believed I loved you all year
for that first kiss, for the slant of the snow shadows
that night when your back retreated.

Your name like memory
and loss and love and hate
and regret and redemption.

You shapeshifted like the ancestors did.

You became that lost animal
I sought you as though
I was that huntress
with a thousand guiding spirits on her hip.
Your name was mine and I forgot the sound
of my voice when I saw yours. You are gone
like the blueberry hue of spring
is covered and wrinkled.
You wrinkled in front of me
my dream like a blade of steel
my heart back in that underwater home
where your words I can't hear again.
Where you are lost to me again.

I can't find you anywhere.

Your stranger is behind me and I am running
the deer retreating, your consuming pointing
I had to run.
You are nowhere now.

You are all wrapped up in a dream you had
that was never real.
And now it is yours to eat
until your stomach feels the regret.
And I am the smoke from the cedar burning
the babies in my palm.

Biingeji.

The First Swimming

Milkweed dipping her head.
Silicone prayers.

A sturgeon
Pulled
to giizis

Let me hear your
name
tonight.

Name.
Like sturgeon gasping.

Namê

Tracing our veins
Down soft arms
Naming
And pointing
textual drownings
like the gasping
stillgills
like the breathing
never happened.

A finger
my lips
biting
a species
into history.

Bloodtelling.

Against our walls.
Our books
Open
Name
Dripping
Soft new milk.

Morning, your hands.
Hunters
Gathering their
Tools
Back
From blood.
Body. Mine.
Its mine.
The opening
To creation
You are
entering.

Filling words are
sacred filling
like firewood.

Mommy's hands.
Her hands
older than
treebranches

painting our mornings
backwards
in the breathing.

Big hips
our hips are losing
Language in our
Blankets
Small hands grabbing
the ends
Of things

Mommy's hands bleeding
Babies bodies bleeding
Daddy screaming
Oka's drip.

Cattail-tip.
We smell you
Under him.
We are walking
acorn pathways
while he
drips his body
over our
Silence.

Morning kindling.
We knew we made it.

Milkweed

Somehow the feasting
attached itself to our bodies
gnawing against each others
hungry corners.

Your tongue
birchbark
sliding my
back against the earth
your shoulders
half hiding the moonsmile
and our breaths
are crawling like
broken weavings
in and out of each other.

Isn't firelight created by our touches? Hasn't the wind
    been good
to us to drive our fleshed humming together—our waters
    blending into each
other, our drippings tonguing each other away
    from mourning?

Like a cattail exploding into milkweed
slitting morning away from dawn
we feed eternity with the currents from
our lateral curving
hollowing slicing history apart
through your body, mine
finding truth the waters
swallowing yearning like a
thirsty earth.

Elijah Harper

no: mon'a.

one sound.
rejection. refusal. rebuff.

what does *no* mean?

silenced ignored disregarded
powerhungered this word
shapes action a deconstructing
of want

negotiation and discussion
no shifts conduct
against a tired history.

how many of our people
dreamed of saying no
how many of our people
died with no on their tongues?

construct your soft rejection of
meech lake into
soft syllables that turn
colonialism sideways.

the colour of *no* staining
whitewashed walls
reddripping

one buffalo
mother covering
her baby's deathsong
with her own swollen body.

soft squelching the
final breath
the heaving of finality
the grandmother
burying the remains inaudibly.

and the women
the internal *no's*
the pushing fleshsounds
hipthrust burials
the rust of a lost
no-hum underground.
the table must have been long.
suits pressed, that eagle feather
spreading her length over his palm.

and they watched migizi spread each feathertip
because they wrote her journey into
    our knowing.

Elijah: the Bible
residential school the voices

James 5:17
there was a man with a nature like ours, and
he prayed fervently that it might not rain, and
for three years and six months it did not rain on
the earth.

No, in 1990
not unanimous
that eagle
feather soaked
their clean tables
undetecting rain

ratification
leaking ink
like unsung prayers.

sacred assembly, a promise
hands, a milkweed opening.

elijah the thunderer
the qur'an's great and righteous prophet.

but he is ours
no ownership ahki
Creator—the simple voicing of
prophecy—

no—
a word
more powerful
than
freedom.

no and it was no.
Elijiah.

Mo'na.

Ondaas

Those words, your lips
the deep vein behind your left ear that
throbs like a beacon
I need to hold you.

Daga, all your resistance.
Daga, all your pain
That spooling
the way the kids spill milk
and we get the cloths and lap it up
their little mouths open.

Sometimes you step forward
in words, and
ningiiwanaadiz.
Sometimes we step forward
and words

those words are eaten.

Anishinaabe lovesounds.
We are the crickets in that
cunning morning.
When the fucking and morning collide.
Those little birdies to swat.
Those black things, the morning interlude.
Your hands all in my hair, and I can't look up.

Sometimes morning comes before we can name it.

And its spilling, between our lovemaking,
your hissing at the radio,
the phone, the tv,
the spittling the scratching of my nails
because I left you

ikidon miinawaa:
Say it again.
Say it the fuck again.
Ididon miinawaa.

You find me here, because I never left you.

Desire

stirring, the night wakes
the click of bone a twig inside of firelight
the salmon stilled and all small eyes sleeping
your body is a braid
limbs fingers pubic hair
tucked away wound tight
deeply rooted flesh
the loop and pull and coming together
a woman's hand, faithful

I wear nothing but a basket on my lap
sorting leaves a long vein trailing the edge
of green like an arrow piercing my woman
a wisp of nettle settling on my fingertips
brown hands that weave the dawn

our fire is dying
embers lay flat gasping
my tea grows cold
your stomach rises
a bread lifting a slow yeast
forming

earlier your sweat rose
beads
her hands needling blue and red
threading baubling colour
earrings that glint when she dances
waving like flags
for the feet that walk home
clanging so close to her sound
her feet move quick a voyage

your first thrust a weight
petals bursting the nectar
suckle the moist
your sweat

I tongue it

not recognizing your heat by
the fire
transformed a shifting of
pulse veins on my tongue
your marrow seeping
a weeping of bone on bone
I cradled you later
like one of my babies
head on my breasts
the length of your hair a shadow
that made me think of Delilah
and how she knew about power
and how to steal it

instead I rebraided your hair
my fingers wet
smoothing the ends with our
juices our bodysong
your weight a chant against the
blankets that held us
the tea scent that hovered
its sage waters
birthing quivers and little
songs that I hummed against
your dreaming

lightning and your body jumps
leaf tips edge my thumb
I listen for a beat of rain
see the curve of love in the corner
crouching there

a boundaryline beside my shoes
muddy from my shoemarks

when I ran to you
your laughter waiting as sure as
a baby crowning
a weight against my chest
your still lips stained with
my opening
a woodpecker bristled with fine shavings
the falling in its descent
like bristled rain

stirring, the night wakes
and I wait here for morning
your waking
insert my limbs in your braiding
my want a kiln to seal us
so we never leave here again

Rape

Simple.
Breadmaking.
The ingredients:
Flour.
Sugar.
Eggs.
Milk.

Simple.

Limbs.
Panties.
Sweat.
Fear.
Flesh.

Cheekagainstthepillow.
My mother hangs laundry
Her fingers bleeding in the bleach.
She sleeps later, so tired
our clothes
Like rows and rows
and rows of
Little crosses.
So tight and new.
A graveyard of panting.

His face.
A sturgeon plunging
mid-dream
The long fumbling
Of
Fingers
And

Flesh
And
Wiping
His memory
Away
With the edge of
a silent-eared bear
who you
never trusted
again.

She came back
Lips kindling fire
It all
Fell
Crooked
When she did not
see a thing.

The blood spirals
Down St. Marys River
Thorns and birchbark
Piercing
The berry
Of small hearts.

Three:
The world so bright.

Six:
Smudges and I wonder
where they came from.

Hands
Veins
And fingers.

Her mouth beautiful, hair
A golden pathway.

She spread me against flowers.

Legs so hard to bend
Trying to hold them back
My ears pulsing
Want to see her smile
To make her stop
Her smile
My exit.

I thought I never saw anyone so
Pretty until I watched her hold
The blood of my body like a baby.

Startled, the sun
Drumsongs like
Semaa
Lost flavour.

Namê sinking down your
Longing gills
Softening.
Namê: they took me too.

And gave me one after
the other to the other
Until I lost my name.

Sturgeon like a long
Map
Belly
Singing
History.

Mapwalls, I disappeared.

The blood of our women
Pictographs against
A wall of
Screaming
Being
Photographed
Your soft face
Placing
Me in the stories

Of soft clay
And riverblood.

Niibinabe

I have learned to write from all angles.
When we are allowed to speak, understand
without writing or performing for cultural insistence
from a particular audience.
This is the Anishinaabe woman and stories.
Just for stories. For words.
Diving into them.

Pulling the life and darkness from the bottom
strange and beautiful waterbed, just like in Creation.
How many missing and murdered Indigenous women
    are there?
The media and reports estimate around 600.
Families and memories speak thousands and thousands
until our lips are closed.

Limbs sprawled like tree-roots.
Nibi's mouth parting
showing the bottom of the river
all her guts exposed.
Imagine a body formed and alive and thinking
and spreading her fingers across the earth
—span in living.
Making a life. Making small gestures to
show what she is thinking.
Her babies watching her
movements as significant as breathing.
Like she might know everything.
Her babies forming the
half cusp of sky around her—
the other side already filled by
the weight of history.
Imagine a woman. Your mother.
Imagine a woman that
created your first stories.
And then she is gone.

Just gone.

Just.
Gone.
Just.
Gone. Apani.

We are
the hanging threads of these stories.
I am the daughter of memory.
Of mothers floating.
Of mothers tangled in cattails.
Bounded by history
Legs wrapped, hands tied, hair pulled
breasts purpled, mouths gagged
With history's rank scent.
The stench of vacancy.
Of yarrow staining the lost mouths of
Tonguing a future.

Privilege is the screwdriver lost in
Betty Osborne
Not the hand
The residue that must listen to her story for centuries
Those years steeped with questions
this handle placed in a plastic bag
her blood memory
Seeping into its making. Having to listen now forever.
You cut her womb in half, so listen. Yellow-edged and
    shivering
These words and our moving bodies are all we have left
    to give you.

How does a country endure on top of piles and piles
    and piles and piles
Of disposed women's bodies? How can a conscience
    persist here?
Dissonance, like arduous, imploring flesh
Pants ankling like a prison
Faces painted like petroglyphs, seared into the earthface.

Flakes of skin embedding onto ahki
and screams pouring out of the earth's drilling, blood mixed
   with oil and soil
And soaking into footsteps like moans
Giizi watching, recording
These women
Into Canada's writhing landscape.
I come to you in a loud silence
DEBWEWIN screaming.

And this is where I create a
Throatsound so that you might understand.
Gdi-nweninaa.
That knotted presence.
The whole thing.
That steep price of meat
But only the best cut.
Do you remember your finest meal with your families?
Well, I do and it sounded like fire.
When we ate it.
The very tip that just might float above you
unless you sucked it down
Fast

That river always finding things
And keeping them as her own?
The mermaid.
Those stories of that woman-fish
which pokes her head up every
Decade or so?
Those sightings.
The Nibinaabe.
The windigo.
That rock you skipped, and never saw again

But the story that you held on to?
She is here.
Tracing herself up your footwalls
Our bodies making
A hollow home
For memory to burrow in
Mounds
And mounds
Of
Open highway.

It's really small this memory. It's nothing at all. It's the
    pinprick
That broke the rest of the memories in half. It is nothing,
    really.
Just the center of all rolling and moving things.

His cock swam like a sturgeon. So copious.
Do you know how large sturgeons can grow?
The biggest fish, that is why they sustained us for centuries.
Name. Nameo. The largest fish.
One which slices the narrow skin of water apart.
And they went missing.
One by one by the dozen, but the thousands
their bodies writhing in zhaagonosh hands—currency.

The sturgeon aren't as big as they used to be in our waters.
Nibi.
Maybe they are afraid to go
to be sighted
the remembering.

Sometimes I think the sturgeon are like our women.
So many lives stuffed and sliced and poured like oil
On top of drowning waters.

Can waters drown?

Nibi thirsting.
Nibi drowning on her own desire to persist.

Mouths little hungry
Vestibules
trying to swallow every fucking thing in sight.
Spreading lips, spreading them open.
Pink labia so soft it is like silkweed on the bottom of
     the ocean.
Those soft hummings—those spinepulls—
Those seconds you've searched the air, and no one's there.
Windigo.
The turning.

And you think and you think and you think
and you think and you think and you think.
And you don't know where it came from.
Windigo.
That soft pulling of eyelids
The tree shaking
The under.

That placid place
Where all sounds endure.
Nibinaabe.
Under
Under under under under under under
Ground.
and the water place lurching the watching

The choking and leaving the dead things hidden
Like they were never here at all.
Until you see a tail edge underwater, a slight
Shiver on the cusp of the surface.
Those sturgeon are persistent in their subsistence, aren't they?

Like nibinaabe
Those murky stories.

Morning

rows and rows
like fences like jagged teeth like a foggy horizon
of mountains pressing into each other as lovers do
when leaving
they stand

some so small they look like children
some so bent they look like old women
some so beautiful that they need to be in a picture to
stop the aging that hurt brings to end the presence of the
approaching men to end the hands that spread their
    flesh open
as wide as moosehide after a skinning
left rotting and flapping in the near night

the sound of a hoof hitting a fat maple like a gunshot
   in the night

a song of death that keeps the children awake
fearful and watchful for morning
with its low winds and birdsongs that disguise
the brutality of the night

rows and rows
like totems
varying faces and memories painted over them

eyes that watch the passerby for a sign a hint of interest

watch for glinting watches or brand name shoes
eyes that understand the persistence of history
the simplicity of abandonment
eyes that can strip the suit of colonialism
piece by piece from a morning on the street

and stand there in their rows of concrete
reminding me of pine boxes and bones with living flesh
and dying flesh and the forsaken eyes of so many sisters

lined up and for sale and believing the lies

that no
we were not the women we read about
were never them
they did not exist
if they did
they were just stories to soothe us
to taint our bloodstains
to mock us
to try to make us stronger

they were always us like us like us in rows and rows
like gravemarkers lined and reminding
in bold letters loud and clear and reminding
us to shout out that we do not belong here
on this morning of clear washing waves over our skins
brown and bruised but still breathing and still breathing

each morning after the other and other and other

breath flowing like small creeks we still remember somehow
from childhood that we carry with us like a small purse
filled with things
heavy things in a purse so small under the
lipsticks and condoms and vial of little white pills
heavy things that scream as loud as mourning

a mother that wakes and finds her babies gone

a young girl with blood down her thighs

a grandmother without any daughters left

and a lone woman under a man that she loves
breathing to the drum of one heart
and giving themselves to morning
to wash this all away and return to a place like home
where these things never happen

where men don't take these women
lost in rows and rows of pain
and bury them in the mountains of history
stuffed with limbs and hearts and long black hair
rows and rows of brown legs walking
further and further away from us
a long long way from morning

wanishin. the lost ahki pulsing our cheeks against
the stain of morning, our pressing Nokomis
tearing, our crying, our stepping
into the bland winter without a song
the treading forward anyways
wanishin, her story.

ikway

a sprawl of seed and root
on the blanket
like a feast

we pulled them from the earth
our hands browned to the wrist
fog like sage sitting on our backs
at dawn
fog like a spirit
over us
as we drank the new air
our babies wrapped in morning
sumac brushing their feet
cattails smushed in baby palms
while we worked

our hands sift through the baskets
lifting more to the blanket
green stems and herbs
a ladybug trailing a cusp of leaf
and the children's feet browned
from the dirt
acorns roll back and forth
between fingers
small voices at our feet
hair thick as pelts sweat our necks
burdock piles
scenting skins and fastening their memory
onto our tongues
we work fast
water boiling

braying dogs singing to us through the doorflap

our men return
voices outside running together into a
rumble a rolling thunder

our men return
their sturgeon skin wafting toward us
riverwater laughter warming us

the fires start and the footsteps quicken
noontime and the seeds fall into piles
resting on our palms fingers spread falling
our babies crane their necks fingers trying
to catch the seedlings
baby breaths milkweed
baby breaths until we reach over and stroke their cheeks
hazelnut eyes absorbing our touch
their fingers stroking seed
our hands pressed to the droop of cheek
the low slope of childhood
gurgling us to motion

we hold the roots in our palms
stroke their fullness
brush the dirt from their bodies
yarrow thick with plush fullness
yarrow nurtured from the soil up
the rains purifying the root arms the rains
crying into its meat
filling it up branching it into our hands
yarrow brushing our palms
each swipe leaves dirt on our lap
our fingerpads wet with soil
the water boils
rolls and bubbles
steam drips us sweat and steam

hides our faces as we drop the roots into
the water
steam purifies us yarrow air root engulfs
our space
our babies chewing stems beside us
before they sleep
the sturgeon filling the smoke outside
their bodies sacrificed and open
flesh exposed to the midday
like midnight under the moon

our waters take the colours of the root
stems root seed air our faces drench
backs ache from hunching
babies on our breast limbs restful babies
lips like sturgeon pucker the drip of
afternoon the men gather round the fire
singe a sky away from morning steam drowns
the medicine out boils healing surrounding
faces carved stonelike
a lone grandfather sits under a maple
fat with syrup spring hunching over him in
protection
we sing this lifesong boiling we pray this
day in humming we watch the roots giving
their life to us we send the seed toward our
bodies we brush a hair from our babies cheek
remove a wet cattail from the inner palm
and join the men in feasting

day breaks and we gather
the sturgeon waiting the rice plumped
carving life around the fire

the dogs rest while we feast in silence.

mahwee animikee

on a hill black hair flying
her back turned, eyes closed
people say she looked like thunder
if thunder had a face

last we saw of her
first time her husband saw her crying
was when she ran toward that hill
heels blackened from the dirt
black hair flying

that morning, face carved into story
she was talking to me about how the
Ojibway women would just put their men's
things outside the door when they wanted
them to leave
they wouldn't come back in anger
they would just go

go

mahwee

away

mahwee

mahwee

thunder crying is as dense as pelts
hung airborne drying after the rains
the deep of the river the bottom the dank
blackness riverbottom searching under shells
finding seaweed skins and bloodsuckers
digging digging without a breath

the hill sits on the edge of the reserve
beside the trail of tracks
trains pass by and watch the children
picking berries watch the children
chokecherries in palm

on the hill she looks majestic
something from another world
a sky image a carving a long
limbed daughter with tears too big
for her face with tears like armies of
ants journeying their abundance
homeward
she never sits
stands statued the train
whipping her hair thundering
her body raining her with wind
clothes tight around her she is
beautiful she is pained she is grief
and he doesn't follow her he doesn't
follow her

she is last seen there
blueberries crushed on her ankles
legs wrapped in milkweed
dress wet and hair like pillars down back
she is thinking but she can't be read
just watching the train back just watching
its slither its stealth its smooth escape

past mourning she lifts her fists
like lightning lifts her pain to the sky
and offers it outward a bounty
palms so small childlike wrinkled from the rain
a band of gold an orifice a circle a glint
a first flash before the light falls down

quills

unclosed I am naked
bare as otterskin
needy shivered eyespans
so desperate and I cannot find you here
without barriers
a fur of survival
a body of quills that span a lifetime over me
this protection so necessary in the heart of a woman

a child this child with once soft hands
that held babydolls so close and slept with three
nightlights
this girl who still feels strangled and unclothed

I am a woman who sleeps beside you at night
your man's body
your leghairs
layering me and sleep and wake
the nights and days and hours

I become more prickly

an animal guarding up the bushes
an armour finding all these things to hide behind
so many doors and windows and walls
and avoiding the closeness
your touch so near
so drowning
the attentiveness
escaped from the quotidian
your seeking to find me under the blankets
so many the sheets so many pillows on my bed
so many layers over me
skins so thickened those years
the buildup

your hands the unpeeling
and I will let you
I might let you
I might chafe the skin
the veins to bone
the marrow dank
and unappealing
the childhood cells so hollering
so disguised in the forest where I left her
where she still lay
sleeping in the triangles of light

Quiet Path

somewhere between Garden River
and the end of the world
we stopped and plucked the hairs off
the underside of a plant
what is this you asked of me

I shrugged not thinking of healing

but your breath and when I laid down
squishing milkweed my ear heard
insects gratifying the ground
felt sap on your hands when you stroked
behind my neck
little scurries above us
and this wash of land made me
reach for you

grab your backskin and pull you over me

the north on your
breath
the autumn falling down
a loon beside a creek
not far off
my belly still browned from summer
old tattoos greening on my flesh you
are a giver

wanting for me
wanting my breath my tongue to find you but
giving me afternoons beside my country
inside the dirt my legs wrapping
you over me
a spider finding its meat
a drift of air shivering us the sun
casting a prelude to arch me toward it

your mouth is the universe

your sweat as current
a sudden spiral
the throat of
all roots
closing upon us
your fall and the sight of a ladybug over my
thumb is nightfall
the stars playing music
and we go
unsheathing
a betrayal
a leaving
our car starting is dull twanging
a braying outside of a
muddied window
inside the ring

we died before we met
your best suit my shrivelled gown
we were finished before our first gaze
little puffs of smoke under your eyes from
a finished cigarette

we went straight for the killing

my shrivelling turning hard
a grape burnt out by the summer
an acorn's cracking the carcass on an old
reserve road

you went before I did years
buried your
heart so laughing
so light that it did not exist
it disappeared
your crying never
happened

how is it that two joinings
so immediate
so fiery
limbs circling as boxers do
seems so small beside the firelight
beside the hurts that pain like a
simple invitation
that falls like dawn across our bed

ikwaywug

separate we survive
living and living
and our breaths as fire
and wind and we exist here

ikwaywug

women as limbs
and eyes
and minds
rivered against aureate banks
that embrace the currents
steep over us like mother's arms
as long as histories
as tutelary
demulcent as a new birth brings
a feather brushed on cheek
a scream against a petroglyph
birthing images onto us

a womb expulsing thought against
thought against
thought
and we are here walking
sumac against our heels
burdock ankling our flesh
stained and greened
brimming against a boiling pot
a tea circling
a yarrow coloured dream
circling us and swallowing
the scathe on our throats
the burn like a brand
a leaf that floats against the cusp
of your cup away from the others
each path a cure or a failure
sometimes a regret

ikwaywug, I hear you.

palm you against my chest
inhale your being and necessity
somehow hale your path onto mine
force your footwalk over mine
somehow breathe your names against
your sigh

forget forgive forget and heal
your stories from my gut and scream your beasts to life
when they wriggle away from me
like a slippery, vibrant baby
exposed to light against an annealed night when
the lake is stilled under the force of the moon
repulsed by the doctors touch
and impressed to survive somehow

I still scream your stories
my voice haggared and broken
and falling a rain of shards
meant to be heard
the kind ran from

ikwaywug

hear me
and join me from your separate paths
we are one
given
the voice our grandmothers carved
as long as the flattened rocks hot with july

dominated by footpaths louder than ours
calm night

unmoving hand
a plain of flesh like a platter feasting us
a night like a preparation
as though the earth is altering me
your soil stamping me thousands of years
the voices so urgent
a history of womansounds still boiling
a rallying of tongues beneath a starlessness
a stillness
a crying underfoot
the world celebrates a land hundreds of years old but
    tasting
thousands
a compression of years like layered bones

ikwaywug crying

an existence that surpasses this façade of fireworks and
stardom
so many women laying still amid the soils
teared and clawing fingernails torn from their flesh
the women laying against each other as cattails
    swaying slightly
in the wind
tipped with moonlight
dancing ancient dances and singing stories that
    overturn
the pressed earth that uncurl the pages of our books

inch outward
like a milkweed bursting forth
frothing and dripping
so suddenly that the birds stop the squirrels jump
    backward
the whole earth shifts
with the magnitude
a shudder over Agawa
the rocks shift

the tourists gaze outward
as though the lake is an irascible sound
the pamphlets damp with tears and they stop their walk
    and know
your song here
understand for a moment the story that got pulled out
    and torn and
blown away

and ikway

your emerging is permanent

a statue
an anthem
a bud
against a scorched rockface
and we lay against the rock like fossils uncovered
a species unearthed
coughing against yellowed pages
the dust in our hair
skin like a fine smoke

bawshinaway

listless smoke
surrender
fingers in mine
I rise   you rise she rises
Nikomis
open the door
pull back the flap
lift the branches
let us waken
and pull our children's bones out and breathe a
breath onto them
kill the indignance
kill the wounding
kill the silence
our mouths a cave of petroglyphs screaming a story
a bare faced rock that no sun can decay that no

wind can erase
Ikway

look at me
see me

assuage me

hear me

take your drum and cradle it like a baby
a spiritchild taken
your womb billowed,
emptied
small cradleboards placed in a corner for the
next generation
for the ghostbabies
that scream like the taken
that cry against the flesh of these trees
that scream a song that no one hears
unless you listen
unless you turn
and part the brush and walk in
and swallow the screams
and decide to speak
take the babies bones and peel the moss back from them,
peel the tongues from the ground and demand
their lives back from the ground
and chew the pages of their lives into a fine silt
and spit them into the tea
and walk away and let them live

bounding the killers
with your silence
an aquiesce that stills the waters
and the tea brews stronger
for all the failing hands

Ikway

your tongue is building with a new blood
no longer curled inside a skull emptied and
entrenched with soil
your tongue is wet with our tea swimming
hundreds of years swimming and broiling
bubbling its leaves over a fire left lit
by a lone grandmother, hunched and dying
her babies bones holding the pot over the fire
bones like autumn leaves under her feet
barefeet browned stained greened
she lit the fire left this fire lit this fire prayed this fire
to life

mushkeeki

and it burnt
each year
new stems fell
new buds fell
new leafs fell

yarrow
cohosh
bloodroot
foxglove
primrose
geranium
goldenseal
hollyhock
jessamine
hyssop
sorell
sage
valerian
turmeric

falling falling

skywoman's open mouth falling
and the cattails rose
they rose they rose
watched over this tea that piled high
grew fertile

new plants falling
fell inside and this tea brewed
a sacred water
prayed over by every nascent tongue
each missing woman's spit and tears and blood
magnified this flame
until the grandmother died
and her bones piled themselves
atop the babies
like kindling

marrow leaking onto the earth
fattening it
bulging it outside of
history's beligerently loosened seams

nikomis
nikomis

your babies footsteps running toward your entry
your babies footsteps running
and nikomis falling
small arms circling
and she succumbs
long hair draped the thousand babies
a blanket thickened and softened
like ripe moss

nikomis, welcome.

for centuries
the tea stills and waits and here
treading of feet everywhere and bones rattle
the marrow leaks onto a tacit soil
and the owls cry silence the deer hover in wait
all the world is sounded in a drifted leaf
and the tea waits
waiting
growing
fattening bulging and stronging

a thick liquid
its boil causing all the creatures to lay in watch
all the creatures to lay their young before it
a baptism
a cleansing
against the bubbling
until it decides to speak.

and the cedar grows
pushes its branches out
exhales its breathes
skins itself
the green tearing open
and the lushness scenting
permeating the deadened stems
the dying plants
fattening the air
with its breath

gishkeekandug

all women inhale.
the girl babies
sense a beating heart
a tentative womb
a thrust of wisp a cusp

of cedar against
a forming lip

gishkeedandug

the petroglyphs
boxed in by glass
screaming to exhale

gisheedangug
ikwaywug

your first sigh is swallowed
and the ancient hand
paused
and the marrow dripping like syrup

ikwaywug drink
whisper your stories
because our screams don't work

sagesong
full with smoke
belly indented inhaled
bellybutton thrust outward

a laboured woman drunk with panic
her sisters lost
and left alone to push, cattails palmed
a birth silenced by fear

milkweed bursting on her back as she falls
the baby's head pushed against moss
labia bursting
small black hairs falling
like offerings against the earth
as soft as the formation of ritual
as quiet as the falling of

skywoman
her flesh screaming against the air

the opened buds below ready to receive her
falling
and the earth accepts
and pulls the blood to root the root to marrow
the marrow to a long history
that cannot exhale cannot exhale
and is ready to rupture
to overturn this tea
fervid

as a rock sunned by decades
exposed to the elements and fading
as quick as a carver's hand
the whittling the shavings the
fingers blurring against a moonlessness
against the throat of a rabbit
newly captured

its legs still kicking
its legs still kicking
its legs still kicking

even after all breath is gone
even after the heart has been
swallowed by the earth

and so she speaks
pungent as a secret
a tea offered every living thing
a thick liquid of sacrifice

protection

a guardianship
over the tongues of all women

Four Stars

the fourth birth
flesh grappling into mine
my sister's hands fierce
fingers as unfamiliar as a starfish
craving for a mussel
abyssal
making the pushing more
foreign as if heard from a
distance
the thrusts of air
bubbly

into me
the tube a silty underwater channel

from here the taste of salt
is unnatural
the bags poured her
bloating me into
the heavens

is it possible to live twice at the same moment?

the sky and seabottom
stars and dense sediment
melted into each other
flapping kelps
stars orbit rippling
keeping a rhythm
attaching themselves
to my body
fusing onto me like
seagrass
a pushing against a tide
too thick in its taking
too wide for its yearning

voices heard from a distance
water and air
the surface an invisible wall
mouths are speaking to me
I try to respond
while my body contracts
I try to whisper
my tongue
hollowed out
a shell echoing into
a small ear listening
a vast muscle bloated
floating offshore
a hardening
my stomach forms a mass
a wave a deep thrust a
pinch from the edge of my sister's
watch my husband is green

he has seen this before but he is green

mouth open a fish gasping air he is
shudder a gasping my back arches
body pushes against my will I
am exhaled the back of my throat
pulsing midwives offering hands
my flesh taking over

the suspension

the last bubbling of breath
trapped beneath the surface
a reddening a panic
the heat my face
wet watered tears the sea salt
the slithering of expulsion

a starfish clutched in my palm
my girl-eyes on my sister
palms together a vast star
enveloping the horizon that
splits the sea from the air

and she cries
hair as thick as the night sky

Okidinan: Her Vulva, Stolen

in watch
a shrivelled mother
fallopian tubes as marrow
reddened and spongy
eyes on the limbs of a baby
kicking its legs
socks folded prettily

she eats and does all of the life things
she is supposed to
rises
the morning a beacon
her skin wet with dream
her husband sleeping
his long back breathing
the breaths of the old
slow and machinelike
but she loves him
and he loves her
even though he never got his son

the yearning is over
the babies she sees playing
under the trees are gone
the knitting needles sent to the
salvation army for hands that
have little heads to cover

akwasasne notes
forced sterilizations
blood wider than the great lakes
our thighs sticky as we
gather

an imaginary cry in our gut
breasts severed wrapped in
cloth
the soaking of our dresses

but no one cries for us

misqqui
misqqui

our tongues are bloated with
    unsaid thoughts
our bellies flat
starved
and stolen

she rubs her bellybutton sometimes
thinking of her attachment to her
    own mother
wondering of the severance
the minute the doctor
makes the cut
leaving her abandoned
carving her own path
his eyes like stone on the mother
and child
his hands like white milkweed
caught in morning
tangled on the cord
struggling to escape
the glint of his glasses
a weapon
startling the baby into silence
while the mother sleeps

sometimes it is all stolen
her bodyparts bagged and
garbaged, while she sleeps
the sleep of the

silenced, splayed, soft spirits
shouldering her to wake
and live, live, live
her babies carried to the
First Mother's hands
wrapped and safe.

Creator waking the women
The loved women
The emptied ones
Wake. They are gone but you
Can live.

The colonized drugged sleeping
the piercing her consciousness
to steal her
wombspace, to place the
throbbing, baby-hungered
mouthing on his white
bloodied palm until it
sleeps and he tosses it
into an unknown
field to die with
the rotting autumn
her groggy face being
told she is ok now wake
wake and hurry back.

That night she sleeps
her ancestors cradling her
birthright beside giizis, those stolen
ones who she never knew.

Dying without birthing
The ones meant for her
Her eyes watching the way the
Night eats and swallows the
Sight of nibi.

Swim. She tells herself.
Swim.

Just find the water.
Nibi will clothe you
Nibi will wrap you up
Like the baby you are.

Nibi has a voice like Mother

Then put your body
Let her hand in yours.

Nibi, come find us.

Cradle, cradle me here.

misqqui
misqqui
on your hands.

Somehow she wakes
Body torn, her body
Emptied.

Nibi, remember.

By the Smokefire

by the smokefire he glows orange
takes on the form of a dream, a vision of
a thousand women's nightbreaths
I don't want to reach for him, don't want to
be the one who is needy
he seems fleshless, a trickster
borne from the earthwomb of this
ordinary night

I try to lose sight of him
maybe I will grow tired of his flickering
body encased by smoke and ashes
maybe I won't feel the hand pulling on my
foot, massaging my leg
inside of the cricket calls and lakewater
lapping

it is only us here tonight he says
only us

his hand moving upward
a black movement shadowed by the
moonlessness, forced by the quiet night
the babies sleeping the long night sky the
pattering of squirrel feet hitting leaf
the vision he sees of me in darkness
the lone fish splash at midnight
the quivering thigh and
earthmusk of my
skin

Five Years in the Rain

Five years after his death I let out a long wail
in his memory,
crumpled behind my steering wheel
when I saw the profile of an old Indian man on
the sidewalk.

The strut of his walk
the cheekbones
of my father pierced into my present
a scent of sage and hazelnuts and old spice
screaming like a ghost trailing my mindskin
against my throat, (those old names screamed, his face, his name
I am pawing the place where you last left the plate for the spirits
My head against an emptied plate, because you hand was there)

I loved you and never told you.

I watched the way you spoke and walked and
Watched and watched and watched and wanted you
To see my eyes and for you to look back at me and
Look back at me and look back at me

And all you had to do was smile at me.

Not even smile.

All you had to do was see me there
Even if you were angry.

As long as you saw me there.

And even if you never saw me there
I was happy enough that my
Shadow covered yours.

As long as we met in this lifetime.

The waiting for your eyes on mine was too long.

Eye-chasing, the little awkward, white child
I needed to you to see me, even once.
Even once.

I used to watch you sleeping, thinking you might
Remember in your dreams that you made me
That your body made me, and I, too, am yours.

So, Daddy, when you died, somehow I believed you
Loved me too, even if you didn't

Remember my face.

I held your hand that day you died
Watched that mouth open
And knew you felt me there
Tears over the chipped left tooth

Remembering stories you told us while we
Watched you, my brown sisters on your lap.

I still heard you, even though you never held me.

(Blankets over my head, ashamed because I did not look like
 My sisters. They got to sit on your lap, and I never did.)

I am forty, and still want to be able to walk up
To your chair and crawl up on your lap
And for you to look at me, and pull me up
And put that tattooed brown arm around me
And let me rest there
Against that heartbeat that is mine too.

Forty years old and fantasizing about
The hug that never happened.

And he left, nibo.

Nibo, you left us.

After everyone left, I put my lips on
That fresh dirt and

zaagi'idiwin. This love.
zhawenim. For you.

I never minded looking into those eyes
Even if you never loved me.

Funny thing: I remember how you held your fork,
And how you ate, how you chewed, how you coughed,
How you laughed most of all, how you stood up
Straight when someone was approaching,
How your eyes crinkled at the corners before you
Told a joke when you were getting ready, how you
Chopped wood, how you would throw my sister in the
Air and catch her, how you would sometimes scream in
The night, how you were so strong, and would
Make everybody laugh, how those crinkles beside your
Eyes never rested.

How my sisters hands in yours looked, and how I knew
She felt safe. And I knew that she was special.

How bad I wanted mine there.
How bad I wanted mine there.
Daddy, I wanted mine there too.
Even one time, I just wanted to hold
Your hand and feel safe.

I haven't seen your eyes in over twenty years, but I still
Dream that you might come back and hold my hand.

his gravestone unvisited another year
his words louder this time
of spring
his earthsong a steady companion to the
rain on my windshield
the downpour the quick drenching
of my world the scrape of the wipers
a calm drumbeat
as I scour the rearview mirror for my Daddy's face
along the sidewalk

the small rows of even teeth
the battlescars
the reckless laugh
the buckskin
coat with small tears down the left side

but he is gone
and I coast into a parking lot
abandoned, folded into my seat
frightened at how long it has been since
I let myself think of him
scared of the return

wailing like a child inside of a slaughtered family

angry at the rain for falling so loudly

angry at the night for being so dark that I can barely see

angry at people for killing us slowly and

angry at the world for letting strong Indians die quietly.

Memory

ran home with salt in my mouth
somewhere down in my throat.
trying to pull tangles out of my hair all the way.
long hair, heavy like a pelt
gathering sweat beneath it.
the heat coming from somewhere but the air
the heat pushing like birth out of me
the heat eating my insides into mush.
somewhere a baby is sleeping, I think.
sleeping little minutes of life into unremembered
    bits of dream
its mother nearby, watching babybreaths rise and fall.

pebbles underfoot and I forgot my shoes.
red ones with the blackened soles worn through just enough
and I forgot them
and I know that someone will never notice them
by the thornbushes beside the water
under the pine trees that line so straight upstream.
they will never be found and I knew that I would never
    go back to get them.
salt in my mouth that makes me think of sore throats
my mother forcing me to gargle eight times in the morning.
not the good soupy salt, a sick, sharp salt.

sometime later in a dream
bare voices without a face, without flesh
without a place to live
little hisses that trail over the trees
the snakey path around my house
the long, blue sky of spring:
shewonttell sheisquietlikeaninsect
shewillgohome tosleep andwakeupwithout amemory.

the point between the now and memory
the split second of recognition
is like a pinprick from a thorn
before you watch the blood drip onto your palm
before you reach for a flat, dry leaf to stop the flow
before you run home to a bed that never felt like yours
with hair so thick that the heat never leaves it
blanketing a mind and body
wet with lakewater handprints
and the picture of chimney smoke from your house
above treetop points
that never end.

Grandma, in the smoke

surprising now, this flood.
spring again, but stronger.
these new rains seem to wash
into history acting as the elusive
eraser, mimicking whitewash to
an old girl, and I am silent in my
cleansing.

turn now, spread the smoke thicker
there, over her head, shoulders.

the grandmother clicks her tongue
chews on her cheek, throws
tobacco on the fire.

I sink into her flesh, familiar, bare.

new things aren't frightening here.
this place filled with old voices
laughing me into comfort.
the rain down my back, my long, low spine.
somewhere, the Creator sends more
and I, like a leaf, open to receive it.

tell me the secrets here, Grandma.
please.
remember me? I was six staring into your
coffin, thinking how your cheek looked like
syrup.

my girl, my girl.
that deep laugh like my
father, but with a touch of woman in it.
womanliftedwindy.

she died quietly
with no thoughts of goodbye.
just slippers
beside the bed and a box of small things that
no one understood.

rains picked up toward storm and yet no
trace of home.

somehow, she connected with me.
threw her
scents toward me for years until I found her,
traced her under her tall pine tree where she
would sit quietly wondering where the good
days went.

and I began to speak.

do you remember me watching you?
young enough to hide under the table
while you salted your soup
the yard filled
with legs of all ages

hot sun and corn soup and the chickens
too tired to run straight

and your silence.
just the clicking
and the eyes seeing everything.

my girl, my girl.
take in what you can.
you are drenched, lost in the memories.
breathe in what you are owed. Take your
fill and search the earth for more.
take the small things and hold them in
your heart. Spit out the leftovers for the
earth to eat.

turn now, spread the smoke thicker
over thighs, legs, tired feet.

my history recedes back toward the
water. and I distance myself for a
while, the present pricking me into
a tight fear, my son's generations too
close for me to explain, the feeling that
of a creek after rain, when the frogs first
come out, and twigs float unstuck
over pebbles and rock points.

now she is gone, lost in the smoke.
I like that. when one steps into the full
body.

just the cheek click and I don't see her again.

Oka Eyes

he got new eyes in Oka.
we never saw his old ones again.
we looked for them in the mornings
under the steam of his coffee
behind his papers, over the
long, chipped wood table.

his face was still the same.
lined slightly, though the edges stopped
crinkling and the insides grew harder
like the little black rocks that we
threw from our slingshots.

when he quit his job, the people started
coming. newsmen and the cameras
who he'd shout to over long
conversations where I'd fall asleep to
my head against my sister's arm.
the next day he was on the front page
blasting his old government job, the
one he loved the year before.

people would stop outside our house
and take pictures of my daddy's sign.
Remember Oka it read and at first
people beeped when they passed.
or sometimes threw bottles.

that sign made me nervous.
it made people ask me questions
that I was too young to answer.

a rainstorm chipped away a corner
two years later, and the paint faded.
he climbed up and repainted on the
next dry day.

chin out, eyes wet, red band covering
old army tattoos.

one day the beeping stopped and daddy's
Oka eyes went blind, but the sign stayed
there, barely hanging on, until it blew
away one november night, leaving a long
board-piece weaving back and forth like
an upstream salmon.

I thought I'd be happy that it was gone
but I'd stare at the empty spot
feeling the death of my father's laughter
the root of what's inside a warrior
and his blind eyes would stare at the
direction of the signpost, nodding at the
splintered backdrop.

and I watched his profile, wondering
where the sign landed, dreaming of piecing
it back together before he somehow knew.

we never found the sign, and his eyes
never opened one day, but I still look for
that sign in ditches, mountains, river-edges
knowing its death is as certain as daddy's
old eyes sitting on the edge of Oka
dusted and discarded, but never forgotten.

Inside Your Sweetgrass Hands

safe here somehow
hearing a child's low hum

He's got the whole world in His hands
He's got the whole wide world in His hands
He's got the whole world in His hands
He's got the whole world in His hands...

thinking of the colour of those hands
that hold all of us
even the unwanted ones
the ugly ones with scars and birthmarks
and little freckles that can't be picked off
even the old indian woman that rides her
bike through the reserve highway, cars
beeping, swerving, catching her nylons
in the spokes, but never stopping, never
looking at anyone even when they laugh
and point and throw cigarette butts at
her gray bike with the child's handlebars
her grocery bag balanced there somehow

but we are safe here in those big hands
that I think are the colour of hideskin
but only when it is dry, a softened
burnt summer cattail stem
a side of an acorn
a dull hue of deerfur poised before flight
the underside of love
a cavern filled with sudden light
smeared winter syrup over snow
the tinge of a slow awakening

and they are warmer than before when we
were hated and we were tired and we were
in hiding when we could only see the
blur of shutting doors, the windows inside
of the storm, the traces of our children
disappearing and the aftertaste of death
on our hands, but things are
returning to us, the stolen things are
finding their way back, down your
long fingers and back to us, drifting like
the dreamsmoke of sweetgrass, and we
like it here, the wake, the slow stretch of
late morning, a long yawn after hibernation
the feast after the wait, the waiting, your
fingerpads swollen from our restless slumber
bloodied from our violent dreams

but I still believe you love us
and made us strengthened
kept our eyes alert when the world
thought us dead, forgotten
kept a hungry beating in our ears
made us whisper the truths to our children
over and over and over until they
pulled us up, ripped our flesh that fused itself
to your handskin, forced us to open wide
while the world watched, alarmed by
our rebirth

and we are safe here somehow.

Mothersong

quiet. quiet.
the words of pain won't come.
can't force them out.
I let them eat my insides raw.
I let them starve my tongue.
invisible breath, my chest barely rising.
feel death welling up in this place
coming at me slowly, barely
having to move because I am making
it too easy. I never thought mine would
be a quiet death, me who shrieks with the
break of day, me who once killed a jumping
fish with a rock-edge, me who looked a bear
in the eyes and didn't move until he walked
away. I thought I would die last of all
my sisters, with a wail of courage, with a
shout that made the acorns tremble.

but I am quiet. quiet.
the birth pains stole my words
hold me gripped in their long spasms.
my sisters surround me, pour soft words
over me, use their long, brown fingers
on my feet, pulling the blood down
scenting my forehead with the buds of
my youth, burn sweetgrass in the corner
whisper to one another, chant, chanting
singing me a birth song, eyes calm
not fearing this death, this tearing of
my flesh, this eating of my strength.

quietly, I shift my hips, narrow hips
with no padding to hold a child, strong
from years of running, strong with the

103

sinew of all of my grandmothers roped
into one, strong enough to hold a man
but this child inside has made them quake
but this child inside has claimed them
locked them into submission under her
rapid fish movements that make me
afraid, not for her, but for my future.
she is stronger than me now in the birth.
she has shown me death in the corner
hovered behind the sweetgrass mask
making me see shapes shifting in the smoke
dark shapes that I am not familiar with
but who I know want me for their own.

quietly, I feel my sisters preparing my womb
feel warmth over my thighs, think it is them
pouring a waterbath over my legs, feel my
life shrinking under the pulse of my child
feel my lifeblood being handed to the girl
who I know will not be like me, because
I saw her in a dream and she sung quietly, and
stored my stolen strength around her heart to use
here and there because she will need it someday
and she won't remember her journey out of me
she won't remember how she came to be
or how she quieted her mother named
shechangesfaces, silenced her like a river-
pebble, made me watch and wait for something
in the corner, quiet, quietly.

sisters singing, louder now, some laughing
softly with their shoulders, some serious, I
try to inquire their faces with my eyes as my
tongue has been leadened down from the birth-
effort, my screams have been raging inside, my
heart pulsating with the effort, wanting to push
everything out, the cries, the tears, the tremors of
my girl-baby, who comes slowly, slicing my
wails apart into dust that settles in my throat
dry pants to my ears like a thirsty moose

and I turn my head and try to eat the earth
anything to stop the sounds of broken pain
but my auntie leans forward, scenting my tongue
with rainwater, dusting my hair with smoke
whispering morning to me with her lips
soft gurgles by a new spring brook, an
awakening, a perfect bud balanced on a branch.

and I understand that I will live.

death shrivels in the corner, disappointment
smelling like a fire full blaze, and I breathe in
and out and in and out, my mind opening
to the life around me.

I see them all gathered outside by the fire
telling stories of their own birthings, their own
first gatherings. I see dark hair down backs, some
braided, some loosened for the occasion, I see
shoulders free with laughter, I see lips singing
this new soul into our world. I see the moon
balanced over them, purity dancing through
their union, and then they turn to see my first
wail, my tears blurring them away from me
the taste of blood between my nose and throat
a sound of daybreak lifting me to my feet
the womanfeet around me, gathered, touching
humming me upward, their strong arms lifting
me, lifting me, the weight of my baby trying to
keep me down, lifting me higher, positioning
my feet over a cedarbranch bed, the waft of
cedar enticing me to push, the smell of woman
encouraging me forward out of the circle of girlhood
my baby girl an eel inside me, my stomach shifting
my long hair a forest hanging over the shoulders
of all of my sisters, my mothers, my wise
grandmothers, the musk of a thousand breaths
a hundred limbs entwined.

and then my wail ends, and hers begins.

HER LIFE

a birdwing brushes her cheek the first morning.

I take it as a sign of her new flight
and I am excited by her possibilities.

I show her things. The long veins in leaves
her baby finger trailing them like a path
my hand guiding hers.
she watches our exchange, gurgles
at my words.
I give her words.
before her birth, I spoke to my belly
but now, her eyes moving through our
world, she gathers images, inhales life-
scents, indulges in the careful study of
my face, the tree edging, our shared sky.

one day, she speaks.
mama, mama...her hand in my hair.
little fingers the colour of autumn
breath on my neck, milkweed and
juniper, cheek on cheek, a curve of
cloudskin.

she begins to show me things.
twigs, cattails, ripples in the morning
pond, her long silences, tears at the
death of spring, brown legs through
fields at summer's peak, her drawings
in the sand at nightfall that stay all year
how she sings to moonlight, and always
the sound of love, the sound of love
a fearful sound of love.

she grows through all this.

her aunties like to dress her for dancing.
long quills thudding together, the buckskin
on her calf, her chin up, and small breaths as
she gets lost in sound, the drumbeats
the thickened drumsongs, her own soft song
and I watch her dance away from me.

she sleeps and all is well. moonlight
spreads over her, dreams dance through her
and I watch her face against her arm
memorizing every lash, every twitch
and I turn to my husband, wondering at
the life we've been given.

thank you, creator. chi migwetch.

HER TAKING

autumn again, a slight chill.
firelight and silence.
the scrape of a squirrel's claw
on birchbark.
I hear a woodpecker from the
riverway, a long call of the train.
my husband is gone logging up north.
my girl is asleep, lost in her dreamscape.
I rise and go to sleep, fall asleep to her breaths.
it must not yet be morning because
the day is barely pinkened.
the cabin is cold, my hand hot against
my nosetip. The footsteps come next.
the shuffling.
the long steps that make me rise up.

hard thumps against nearly frozen ground
and not my man's soft footwalk.

my girl does not stir, but I am to my feet
hand raised for battle, my arm reaching
toward a long, wood stick, and I freeze
confused by what I see.

two men, black suits like in the town
in my cabin, their eyes not seeing
moving toward the floorbed where
we sleep, coming toward me like
two bushbears, not stopping, moving
toward us, thumping against the nearly
frozen ground, and my mind cannot
move as fast as them, cannot find a
reason for them to be here and not in
the town, and I wonder if I am still
dreaming, but for their eyes on my baby
their hands under her arms and her small
neck rolling back in loose sleep, and
the size of his hands on her body, and
the other one pushing me away from
her, and I hear ripping and tearing and
I hear a waterfall and I hear a forest
screaming, every howling thing in my
ear and scraping, and floordirt flying
and my hands clawing up his leg
my teeth on his thigh, the heat of blood
against my throat, and the growl of rage
and my little girl screams and my hair
pulls back, my face is covered by a hand
and I can't see her, just a brown leg
kicking and a big hand carrying her out
the door and her eyes and her eyes and
her eyes on mine and I run and they are
gone in a black truck, smoke dripping
my eyes and her eyes and her eyes and
her eyes never leave me.

AFTERWARDS

little holes in the wood.
round little holes, spirals.
if I look hard, there is a drift
of wing that could be seen right
through. If I look hard, some
sudden motion can catch me.
I lay here for days, waiting.

and she never comes back.

my husband says he found me
on the floor beside the bed
shivering, waiting, waiting.
he saw the priest in the outskirts
of town. the father told him
how all the indian kids were sent
out to school.
said they would come back.
said they would learn things
we couldn't teach them.

my cough began before the first
frost. rattled me to sleep, into
dreams where the owl cried to me
where he told me things I didn't
want to hear. into dreams where
I would watch the kids line up
dressed as rabbits, waiting to be
skinned alive.

that owl whispering to me.
things I didn't want to hear.

my ears pounded drumsongs to me
painful ones, with trickles down my
neck. a dark weight on my chest.
little whispers in my ears. Sometimes

my girl's voice, a small cry, and I
would roll over to her cold spot on the
bed, forgetting she was gone.

the fear began to eat me.
I let him, dreaming of death
looking into every corner, begging
him to come back for me, hearing
baby footsteps, night screams,
little girl laughs that make me
crawl to the space between log-posts
and scour the forest, screaming out
her name.

mornings my husband tries to spoon
me soup, bannock bits, wave tobacco
over me, but I fight him off as a
wounded bird, pecking at his hands
making sharp sounds deep from my gut.

soon, he gets my sisters, bring
them to my bed. they gather
sing old songs, lullabies, mother-
songs which make my shoulders
shake with a surge far from death
songs which make a bear emerge
from my memory, an old fire
brought low, brightening.

the women surround me.
wrap me tightly in cloths
run springwater over me, spread
goldenrod around me, fan me
into a quiet sleep, the men outside
around the fire, drumming me
back to life.

my auntie reminds me of stories
of our children, of happier times.
sings me footsteps that I think of
as a dream or memory, feeds me
slivers of love, whispers her name
to me gently, cleansing me back toward
love, the hate seething, the black
flashes of my hand grips on wood
and if I moved faster, and if I fought
harder, and if I didn't go to sleep with
such peace that night, if I was less
quiet, she would still be here.

my chest rattles and the women
place wet cotton pieces for me
to suck on, pull the medicine out of.
I dream of a beavers tail carrying me
somewhere familiar and a small hand in
mine pulling me under shade from the
heat of my thoughts, the scorch of my
present, the ember of sudden disaster.

one day I wake and cry for a long time
and then I eat, my foot tapping in tune with
the men's drumbeats, hearing dull quills
tapping together in another world, a far
off hollow sound, a core of silence, a
heavy thudding, bone on bone.

and I live here, quietly.
silence, my mothersong sliced
from my voicewalls, stolen.
quiet.

Sunday at the Healing Lodge

thirteen poles, shaved cedar
grandmother echoes
pull me in.

my toes hold rocks between them
flex them outward
I watch pebbles nestle in my flesh like bald birds in
brown, curvy nests.
cool smoothness as breath on flesh the flesh
on earth the heat
the warmth of first milk
the first awakening
a surrendering of
spirit to lifescape
the solid body to house us
this heavy flesh.
I glimpse the first recognition of mother
swallow the full peace in a newness of sleep.

my feet now connect to the ground
a waft of sage to lull me to let me drift with it
in prayersong rising.

I admire the woman-pipe
different than the men's with their extra length.
the hip-lines through the smooth rock
the round openings the continuing softness
that smokes me toward it
a juniper song of welcome, a summer story
in my ears only.

and the tobacco falls from my fingers
and the tobacco falls to the rockbowl, scatters.
and the tobacco leaves my flesh, my fingerpads
warm a pillow pulsing rising

while the women sing the morning
throats pushing smokethreads upward
a drop of memory: my mothers eyes in love
curled flesh on flesh a vein of surrender
a continuum of nurture the child in my arms
my lips on his cheek his lashes blinking my tears
my motherblood freed, a new song created.

Anama'e e-mazina'igan:
Prayerbook

Milkweed dipping her head
Silicone prayers
A sturgeon
Pulled
to giizis

Let me hear your
name
tonight
Namè
Like sturgeon gasping
Names
Tracing our veins
Down soft arms
Naming
And pointing
textual drownings
like the gasping
stillgills
Like the breathing
never happened.

A finger my lips biting
A species
Into history.

Bloodtelling.

Against our walls.

Our books
Open
Namè
Dripping
Soft new milk.

Morning and your hands.
Hunters
Gathering their
Tools
Back
From blood.

Body. Mine.
Its mine.
The opening
To creation
You are
Entering.

Filling words are sacred filling
Like firewood.

Mommy's hands her hands
Older than
Treebranches

Painting our mornings backwards
The breathing

Big hips our hips are losing
Language in our
Blankets
Small hands grabbing the
ends
Of things

Mommys hands bleeding
Babies bodies bleeding
Daddy screaming
Oka's drip

Cattailtip. We smell you
Under him.
We are walking acorn
Pathways
While he
Drips his body
Over our
Silence.

Morning kindling.

We knew we made it.

The Wanting

This entering
Your grabbing a vise of insistence
Pulling the librarian out of the long stacks of bookends
A handful of hair wound like a boxer the twirling
Rainbows of my lips
I bend
Against your smooth, hardened chest
Sucking the ends of your fingers
Our pieces a chorus against December's mid-song
Find me here my wet body wearing tight constraints
Pussy icing your strumming a fucking of birds
Two necks wound around the other
Pecking for some unpluckable shard.
And your cock points me to follow.
I do out of an ordinary curiosity, your organ a
Streetsign
A blinking light that directs traffic
And so hungry, I follow you into our bedroom
Filled with our particular things that
Scream our life together like a banner
I already know you beyond your stories
Know you deeper than my own flesh
Your thrift store painting hovered above our heads like a
tombstone
Cock ready you pull me into you expecting my pussy to burst open
And it does because I'm hungry and I love your voice
Like the language of your thrusts
Like the conversation of all our yesterdays
I love you still, more, more now
And so the fucking
Our tired, morning fucking we are trying so hard we have
The naked bodies pointing
blood riding against your blankets
You plunge your hand inside
Our stainings on that clean white towel —

We should have sprawled it against the walls
Painting a still wall canvas with blood and cum and

Saliva and the knowledge of our broken mornings
We should have slung the mire against the mirrors
Smearing the sex breaths deep into
A memory that can be cleaned off
With paper towels and your union t-shirts
My pussy screaming the red screams of the wounded
Wrapping like Christianity around
The throats of the choir
And I like it and I want to tear your spirit
Out of you and watch you bleed your memories into my mouth.
Littlewhimpersyourskintastessharpmymouthyourtonguethelongpush
And I try so hard to cum but you pull away
And I am okay because of your comfort
Your deep need to talk
The talking
After fucking
Your talking
Makes me remember the strong migration of flight
And little words against our pillows
And how I will remember my
Wanting of you.

Us

slice of curtain
the vertical crooked sound
is a long rock being
barraged by a constant
sunning.
shifting the motion into
permanence —
I hold you there.

as quietly as forgiveness
sells its weighty hand.

you stand as still as death
must stand when it marches
toward the tender body

and the deceit in your promise
smells as strong as
the dankness of the late spring
when the milkweeds
bow their mighty
heads onto the ground
ripping
widely open
earthsounds suckling
the last of their
flowing

This is us
Waiting for a cure.

Our sickness a marriage
of burying
ripping up the bones
and suckling
the marrow dry

a drying weed
upside down
watching the
trails through a
rainstained window.

Waaban: Our Bodies as Resistance

I have spent the words like currency, threw them out there and now they sit in buried chambers and I will let them. Once they are freed from my heart, they are like little birds or someone else's prisoners. At least I released the language and your hands tried to catch the words, the fluttering symbols, like falling snowdrops you caught them, melting over your skins like they were never there. Skins are hard to shed for some people. Some people wear the same skins for years over their shoulders, the weight like centuries over them and I watch you do this, your smile faltering. But it falters as though not at all, just a slight drip of the fabric of your cheek. I think of Anaïs Nin and Henry Miller, of their subtle violence, of their outrightness, of their shrewd connections. I don't think of June, who must have felt the solitude of nights against the cheek of her arm, the long waiting, the easy sleeping of one who doesn't ingest the passion of the moment. I think of Anaïs's mouth and the words on her fingertips. Her mouth is redness like the ochre of my people's rocks. Her mouth is redness like a rage and I am forceful in my writing, pulling the words from a grandmother's same redness, of a different hue, from the opposite side of the world, countless years later. Ochred silence, a sturgeon's slow dip, the dip of midnight's throat.

Sometimes basking in dreaming, filtering inside of a warm morning, there is silence. And I think of silence like a droplet, like a secular gift, like an armour against the rush of people, the gale of a long lifesong. You come and I open. There is a parting of ancient seas when you come to me, there is an instilling of my grandmother's songs somewhere, the bones of me are wakening, all marrow expands and I am newness, a hummingbird suckling, a woman waking, limbs and face exposed to the sky.

Your hands are like a chiseler. Quick and inside of the moment. Your scent is a cedar-brimmed sageness, a humming of flesh, brisk walkings toward me, and my gasping is like the sturgeon's riversong. My gasping is an inhaling of the flesh, so much yarrow inside of you, your body like cattails pressed and pressing against my cheek. When I come to you, I already know you like I know the earth. Your body is rooted in the earth that birthed me, your body is rooted in the trees that sway like a storm overhead and I taste your earthen husk inside of my throat, your body tensing like a thick rod for my lips and I love you for a moment and I want your want your possession and I want you under my own flesh this moment. You watch me, and I watch you back. And ahki moves.

Somehow the earth responds. It harnesses me, a grip so primordial it smells like the inside of the spirit when earthbound. A milkweed bursting open, its breath escaped into the morning air and I watch the journey of scents searching for a place to land, and so I swallow it and the consuming is a tearing of pages, a historical laying out of flesh long forgotten. Connected, and the watchfulness is overwhelming. The bodies and the tongues and the singing is a moonsong that is pulled from the pathways that underlie all breaths of the first dreamers, the pure song that hums our heartstrings. The watchfulness expands and in our falling, you press your strong body into me, until we are dancing together with the hum of the earthbeat and we are pressing like morning presses against the night sky, with the persistence of language, the persistence of a radiant dawn that resists the language of everything but your body and mine. Our bodies are our resistance. Waaban. We stay here. Waaban bathing us slowly, her eyes finding our bodies and as slow as creation, pulling herself over us, so we can sleep.

Turtle Island

My mother laid me down on
Anishinaabe soil
Her white skinned baby
that she forgot to pray for.

She thought my skin would save me.

She didn't pray for me like the others.
My veins pulsing skin all my cries
The bark cheeking my beginnings
While she looked eastward
Her family tattooed against her heart

She gave me the soil and my grandmother
Lifted me
Singing
A song
But it never silenced
The history
Weaving itself
Down my throat
So heavy I tilted

Little streams
The body arching.

A man and woman pulled secrets
Out of each other in February
When Ontario shut the doors of reasoning
He held her
And she looked the other way
Her mother raising her deathflag.

And so I built kindness from sticks.

Looking for bears and hugs and eyes
That are windowsills.
And we picked the bugs from them
And sucked matchtips
While we waited.

Baptist uprising we saw
The skirt
Of Jesus

Open arms she held us
Once.
Rocking.
Loud babymouths
Hymning.

Biinjina: inside the body

Bodies stretched centuries wide thinning and yielding slippery
    like clay
Days have no sound limbs spinning and making breaking sounds
Thundering the thunderers cutting the years into segments
    like fire tips
Shkode. Fire voices slicing silence the sharp edges burning
    memory into
Spirit treaties signed in water. Nbiish curling her soft edge, a blanket
Ziibi running like sap in a slow spring, eight fires lined beside her in a
Dream that holds a river screaming upstream into the sky.

Prayer around a long table passed one to the other, used soundlessly
Without caresses, spreading its words against the edge, pressing into it
The easy words the rising sounds the screaming whispers
Holding themselves like a candle, erotic, poised
Limbs braiding each other into reticence.

This heart. The loving.
zaagi'idiwin

pulling in, come in, visit, swimming
the morning, splayed for language
and words to find peace
in this doorway.

Biinjina: the house of stories.

ACKNOWLEDGEMENTS

I want to thank all of those who supported me. Thank you to the Ontario Arts Council and the Canada Council for the Arts for supporting my writing all these years and believing in Indigenous literature. I want to thank my community for being there and being strong. Garden River First Nation is a strong reserve and I am so proud of where I come from. I remember the bridge where I come from that reads: *This is Indian Land*. It was there before I was. I always saw it and I knew that this place — and all these people who came from the same place, and all of those who were here before us — is my home. When I began to consider a title for my poetry, I knew that it came from within my memory, and I knew that I grew from this landscape and so my offerings of poetry come from this Indian land and from this, expanded into my own experiences and babies, and love, activism, and linkages to many, many more voices that came before me. I also acknowledge all those strong sprits who are preparing the future spaces. All those who came before me: chi-miigwetch. Our ancestors are the universe and have our backs and are always there. Mostly, I would never be able to express myself fully without my father, Wallace Belleau, my mother, June Belleau, my sisters, and my children who are my driving force. It ends in my own love, and that is you Paul. You are the very center of my heart. Chi-miigwetch.

Lesley Belleau is an Anishnaabekwe writer from the Ojibway nation of Ketegaunseebee Garden River First Nation, located outside of Bawating/Sault Ste. Marie, Ontario. She is a Ph.D candidate in the Indigenous Studies Department at Trent University in Nogojiwanong (Peterborough, Ontario), and is focusing on studying Indigenous feminine literature, biography and narrative retrieval. She has taught Indigenous Literature, Theatre and Creative Writing at Algoma University in Sault Ste. Marie, and is a T.A. with Marrie Mumford at Trent University in the Theatre Department in the History of Indigenous Dance Theatre.

Lesley writes fiction, essays and poetry and is the author of the short fiction collection *The Colour of Dried Bones* (Kegedonce Press) and the novel *Sweat* (Scrivener Press), as well as other poetic, fictional, academic and blog works, published nationally and internationally. Lesley lives with her five young children and her fiancé.